Retirement Planning for Men

Achieving Freedom and Security in Post Work Life

Ruby Rylan

1

Table of Contents

Introduction

Your New Adventure Begins

A Message to you!!

Welcome to a new stage of life, where freedom and opportunity await beyond the demands of work. For years, you've likely poured time, energy, and dedication into your career, family, and community. Now, you're stepping into a phase that can be every bit as fulfilling and purpose-driven, if not more so. Retirement isn't an end—it's a beginning, a chance to explore who you are without the constraints of a nine-to-five routine. This is your time to rediscover passions, strengthen relationships, and experience life on your own terms.

Adjusting to retirement can feel like standing on the edge of something unknown. Many men find the shift away from a structured work schedule challenging. But here's a comforting truth: just as you adapted to the demands of work, family, and life's ups and downs, you can adapt to the opportunities retirement brings. Think of this stage as a fresh start where each day is yours to shape. You'll have time to reflect on what matters most and set new goals. While this guide will give you practical tools for managing finances, health, and relationships, it also invites you to embrace a mindset of openness, curiosity, and courage as you embark on this adventure.

Redefining Success and Freedom Beyond Work

For decades, success may have been defined by career achievements, financial security, and raising a family. But now, success in retirement means something different: it's about crafting a life that aligns with your personal values, interests, and dreams. Retirement offers the freedom to redefine who you are beyond job titles and daily obligations. Instead of "What do you do?" the question becomes, "How do you want to live?"

Redefining success in this phase starts with knowing what brings you joy and satisfaction. Ask yourself: What makes me feel alive? What activities or hobbies make me lose track of time? These answers can guide your focus. Whether it's learning new skills, traveling, spending time with loved ones, or giving back to your community, retirement allows you to prioritize what genuinely fulfills you. Success might mean developing a stronger connection with family, creating art, volunteering, or simply enjoying each day's small pleasures.

Financial independence plays a vital role here, too. While money doesn't define success, having financial security empowers you to make choices freely and comfortably. This guide will walk you through smart retirement planning, helping you feel confident in managing your resources so that you can focus on what truly matters.

As you enter this retirement chapter, remember that it's okay to take your time. It's normal to feel a mix of excitement and uncertainty. Embrace it. Give yourself permission to explore new interests, revive old hobbies, and meet new people. You may find that, after decades of providing for others, you finally have the space to care for yourself in deeper, more meaningful ways.

This isn't just about "leisure." It's about crafting a life that lets you be at your best—happy, healthy, and free. Consider this guide a trusted companion on your journey. It's packed with practical tips, inspiring stories, and tools for designing a retirement life that's exciting, rewarding, and uniquely yours.

So here's to this new adventure—may it be filled with discovery, laughter, and a fulfilling kind of freedom. Retirement is your time, and your best days may well be just beginning.

Chapter 1

Setting the Foundation for a Worry-Free Retirement

Assessing Your Current Financial Landscape

Before you dive into the plans and dreams of retirement, it's essential to know exactly where you stand financially. Taking a thorough, honest look at your current financial situation will give you a solid foundation to build on. Here's how you can get started:

1. Calculate Your Net Worth

Start by listing your assets and liabilities. Your assets include savings, investments, property, and retirement accounts, while liabilities might include mortgages, loans, or other debts. Subtract your total liabilities from your assets to get your net worth. This snapshot will help you understand your financial footing and reveal areas you may need to strengthen.

2. Track Your Monthly Expenses

Understanding your current spending habits is vital to planning your retirement budget. Break down your monthly expenses into categories like housing, groceries, transportation, healthcare, and entertainment.

Look at the essentials versus discretionary spending, so you know what you could adjust if needed.

3. Evaluate Your Income Sources

List out all the income sources you expect to rely on during retirement, such as Social Security, pension, rental income, or dividends from investments. Understanding each income source and when it becomes available can help you determine if adjustments are needed.

4. Estimate Healthcare Costs

Healthcare can be one of the largest expenses in retirement. As a first step, research Medicare options and consider any additional insurance needs you might have. If you have a health savings account (HSA), continue to build it up as it's a tax-free way to cover eligible medical expenses.

5. Consider Debt Repayment

Carrying debt into retirement can be a burden on your income. If you have outstanding debts, especially high-interest debt, create a repayment plan. Paying down or even eliminating debt before retirement can free up more of your retirement income for things you enjoy.

Taking these steps will give you a clearer picture of your finances and help you identify areas for improvement, giving you a more stable foundation for a worry-free retirement.

Understanding Your Retirement Goals: Lifestyle, Family, and Personal Growth

Now that you've assessed your financial landscape, it's time to think about what you want from your retirement. Retirement is a chance to pursue passions, connect with loved ones, and grow in new ways. Clarifying your goals can guide your financial decisions and help you design a retirement that's meaningful to you.

1. Defining Your Lifestyle Goals

What kind of lifestyle do you envision? Do you want to downsize and simplify, or are you aiming to travel frequently? Some men dream of relocating to a peaceful setting, while others might want to stay close to family and community. Consider your day-to-day lifestyle—activities, hobbies, routines—that will make you feel fulfilled.

2. Setting Family Goals

Family is often a top priority during retirement. Think about how you'd like to support and spend time with your family. Do you want to help with grandkids' education, provide financial assistance, or create memorable family gatherings? Understanding your family goals will help shape your financial plan and allow you to allocate resources for the experiences and connections you value most.

3. **Pursuing Personal Growth**

Retirement is also a time to focus on your personal growth and well-being. Consider areas where you'd like to grow—whether it's learning new skills, pursuing creative projects, or even starting a small business. Many retirees find joy in volunteering or mentoring, finding ways to give back and stay connected to the world around them.

4. **Creating a Flexible Plan**

Remember that your goals and lifestyle may change over time. Flexibility is key. As your interests and priorities evolve, your financial plan should be able to adapt. Regularly reviewing your goals will allow you to adjust your budget, plans, and investments as you experience new phases in retirement.

By setting clear goals and understanding what you want from your retirement, you're building a vision that goes beyond just financial security. You're crafting a life that allows you to thrive in ways that bring you joy, satisfaction, and peace of mind.

Chapter 2

Creating Your Retirement Income Blueprint

Retirement is about creating financial security so that you can enjoy your newfound freedom without constantly worrying about money. Building a retirement income blueprint is like creating a roadmap to make sure your income supports the life you want to live.

Managing and Maximizing Social Security Benefits

Social Security is a foundational income source for many retirees, so it's crucial to understand how to get the most from it. Your benefits are based on your lifetime earnings and the age at which you choose to start receiving them, with some flexibility to tailor your benefits to your personal situation.

1. Determine Your Full Retirement Age (FRA)

Social Security offers what's known as a Full Retirement Age, typically between 65 and 67, depending on your birth year. You can begin taking benefits as early as age 62, but they'll be reduced for each month before your FRA. Waiting until you reach your FRA ensures you receive your full benefits, and for each year you delay beyond your FRA (up to age 70), your benefit increases.

2. Evaluate When to Start Benefits

Deciding when to start taking Social Security is a personal decision. If you start early, you'll have more years with benefits, but at a lower monthly amount. If you can afford to wait until you reach or exceed your FRA, your monthly benefit will be higher. Consider factors such as your health, financial needs, and other income sources to help decide the timing that best suits you.

3. Explore Spousal and Survivor Benefits

If you're married, you may be eligible for spousal benefits, which can be up to 50% of your spouse's benefit. If one spouse has significantly lower lifetime earnings, this benefit can be especially valuable. Additionally, survivor benefits are available if one spouse passes away, allowing the surviving spouse to receive the higher of the two benefits. Understanding these options can help you maximize the household income.

Investments, Annuities, and Pensions: Making the Right Choices

After Social Security, many retirees rely on personal investments, pensions, and annuities to supplement their income. It's essential to choose the right mix based on your goals, risk tolerance, and income needs.

1. Understanding Your Pension Options

If you have a pension, you'll likely have several payout options. A common choice is a monthly payment for life, but some plans offer a lump sum. Monthly payments provide steady income, while a lump sum might be appealing if you have a clear investment plan. Weigh the pros and cons of each option, considering how they fit with your overall income needs and whether you have other assets to cover unexpected expenses.

2. Exploring Annuities for Steady Income

An annuity is an insurance product that provides a guaranteed income stream for a set period or your lifetime. Annuities can be a good option if you want to ensure a stable income, especially if you don't have a pension. However, it's important to choose annuities carefully, as they can vary in fees and terms. Consulting with a financial advisor who specializes in retirement planning can help you make a decision that aligns with your needs.

3. Building an Investment Portfolio for Growth and Security

Investments like stocks, bonds, and mutual funds can provide growth and help protect against inflation. A balanced portfolio typically includes a mix of stocks (for growth) and bonds (for stability), adjusted for your risk tolerance and income needs. Generally, as you age, it's wise to move towards a more conservative portfolio to protect your savings from market volatility.

Developing a Sustainable Withdrawal Strategy

Having a reliable withdrawal strategy is crucial for making your retirement savings last. A well-thought-out approach will help you manage your income sources, avoid dipping too deeply into savings, and ensure you have money available for the years to come.

1. Calculate Your Retirement Budget

Start by estimating your annual expenses in retirement, including basics like housing, utilities, healthcare, and discretionary spending. Compare these to your income sources (like Social Security and pensions) to determine how much you'll need to withdraw from your savings each year.

2. Follow a Safe Withdrawal Rate

A popular approach is the "safe withdrawal rate," which involves withdrawing around 4% of your savings annually. This method can help you avoid depleting your savings too quickly. However, the right rate depends on factors like your age, health, and the size of your portfolio. Adjusting your withdrawal rate based on market conditions and lifestyle changes can help your funds last longer.

3. Prioritize Income-Generating Accounts

Consider which accounts to withdraw from first based on tax implications and growth potential. In many cases, it's beneficial to start with accounts that have lower growth potential, allowing tax-advantaged or higher-growth accounts to continue growing for as long as possible. Consult with a financial professional to customize this strategy for your unique circumstances.

4. Adjust Over Time

Life is unpredictable, and your income needs may change over time. Periodically review and adjust your withdrawal strategy based on your spending, investment performance, and any unexpected expenses. Flexibility is key to maintaining a sustainable income throughout retirement.

By creating a retirement income blueprint that balances Social Security, pensions, investments, and a sustainable withdrawal strategy, you'll be well-equipped to enjoy a financially secure and fulfilling retirement.

Chapter 3

The Freedom Fund – Building a Savings Buffer

Planning for retirement goes beyond covering the basics; it's also about creating a cushion that lets you navigate life's unexpected twists without worry. This "Freedom Fund" is your financial buffer—a savings reserve that ensures peace of mind, even if surprises come your way. By setting aside an emergency fund and planning to protect your savings from inflation and market ups and downs, you'll be building a retirement that's resilient and truly freeing.

Emergency Funds for Peace of Mind

An emergency fund is a dedicated reserve of cash to cover unexpected expenses, like medical bills, home repairs, or even a sudden need to support family. Having this fund in place means you won't need to pull money from long-term investments when the unexpected happens, keeping your main retirement savings intact. Here's how to set up an emergency fund that works for you:

1. **Determine How Much to Save**

A general rule is to set aside enough cash to cover three to six months of living expenses, but in retirement, consider aiming for at least a year's worth of essential expenses. This extra buffer gives you more stability since, without a steady paycheck, unexpected costs can be harder to manage.

2. Choose an Accessible Account

Your emergency fund should be kept somewhere safe and easy to access—think savings accounts, money market accounts, or short-term CDs. Avoid locking it into long-term investments, which could make it hard to access quickly or result in penalties. While these accounts might not have high interest, the main purpose here is stability and liquidity.

3. Build It Slowly, If Necessary

If you don't already have an emergency fund, don't worry about saving it all at once. Start by setting aside a small portion each month and increase it over time. You could also set aside any windfalls, such as tax refunds or gifts, to help your fund grow faster.

4. Replenish After Use

If you end up using your emergency fund, make it a priority to rebuild it. This way, it's always ready if needed. Think of it as a protective shield for your larger retirement nest egg, helping you stay financially sound even if the unexpected comes knocking.

Protecting Your Nest Egg Against Inflation and Market Volatility

Building a Freedom Fund is one step toward a secure retirement, but protecting your entire nest egg from losing value is just as important. Inflation and market fluctuations can reduce the purchasing power of your savings, so it's essential to take steps to safeguard your funds.

1. Understanding Inflation's Impact

Inflation means that prices rise over time, which can slowly chip away at your savings. What costs $100 today might cost $110 a few years from now. Without a plan, inflation can make it harder to afford essentials down the road, so taking proactive steps is crucial.

2. Invest in Assets That Outpace Inflation

Keeping all your money in low-interest accounts may feel safe, but over time, inflation can erode their value. Consider maintaining a balanced portfolio that includes stocks or inflation-protected securities, which have a better chance of growing faster than inflation. Even in retirement, a modest stock allocation can help protect against rising costs, as long as it aligns with your risk tolerance.

3. Adjusting Your Budget Over Time

Another way to combat inflation is by regularly revisiting your budget. As prices increase, you may find opportunities to cut back on non-essentials or explore more cost-effective options for regular expenses. Small adjustments, like choosing less expensive hobbies or dining options, can help stretch your funds without affecting your quality of life.

4. Mitigating Market Volatility

Market fluctuations are inevitable, but you can minimize their impact by diversifying your investments. Diversification means spreading your investments across different types of assets (such as stocks, bonds, and real estate), which can help reduce risk. During downturns, having a diversified portfolio can soften the blow and give you time to recover.

5. Setting Up a "Safe Bucket" for Market Downturns

Many retirees use a "bucket" strategy for investments, keeping some funds in safer, more stable accounts and others in growth-focused investments. For example, one bucket might hold two to three years' worth of living expenses in cash or short-term bonds, while another bucket is invested for long-term growth. This way, if markets are down, you can draw from your safe bucket, giving your other investments time to rebound.

6. Regularly Rebalance Your Portfolio

Over time, the performance of different investments can shift your portfolio's balance. Rebalancing means periodically adjusting your investments to match your target allocation, ensuring your savings remain aligned with your risk tolerance and income needs. Rebalancing every year or so can help you maintain a steady and resilient portfolio.

By building an emergency fund and protecting your nest egg against inflation and market volatility, you create a safety net that gives you freedom. With these protections in place, you'll be able to enjoy your retirement more fully, knowing you're prepared for life's surprises while safeguarding your financial future.

Chapter 4

Planning for Health and Longevity

Health is the backbone of a fulfilling retirement, allowing you to enjoy your hard-earned freedom and pursue your passions with energy and peace of mind. Planning for health in retirement means addressing three key areas: understanding your healthcare options, maintaining your physical and mental well-being, and preparing for potential long-term care needs.

Healthcare Options and Medicare Basics

Healthcare is one of the most significant expenses retirees face, and understanding your options can help you manage costs while getting the care you need. For many retirees, Medicare serves as a primary healthcare resource, but it's important to know what it covers, what it doesn't, and how to fill any gaps.

1. Medicare Parts A, B, C, and D

Medicare has several parts, each covering different types of care. Here's a quick breakdown:

- **Medicare Part A** covers hospital stays, skilled nursing, and some home health care, typically with no monthly premium if you paid into Medicare during your working years.

- **Medicare Part B** covers doctor visits, outpatient services, and preventive care, but it requires a monthly premium.

- **Medicare Part C** (Medicare Advantage) combines Parts A and B and is offered through private insurers, often including additional services like vision, dental, and sometimes even fitness programs.

- **Medicare Part D** provides prescription drug coverage, helping you manage medication costs.

When enrolling, review each part to determine the right fit for your health needs and budget.

2. Supplemental Coverage (Medigap)

While Medicare covers many essentials, it doesn't pay for everything, and out-of-pocket costs can add up. Medigap plans, offered by private insurance companies, are designed to cover expenses that Medicare doesn't, such as copayments, coinsurance, and deductibles. Investing in a Medigap policy can provide more predictable healthcare expenses and reduce the risk of large, unexpected bills.

3. Evaluate Medicare Advantage Plans

Medicare Advantage plans offer an alternative to traditional Medicare, often bundling additional services. They may also limit out-of-pocket expenses, which can be a financial advantage. Since these plans vary widely, compare options based on the network of providers, extra benefits, and cost structure to find one that aligns with your needs.

4. **Plan for Out-of-Pocket Expenses**

Even with Medicare and supplemental coverage, it's wise to budget for out-of-pocket expenses. Medical costs for treatments, prescription drugs, or specialized care can add up, so having a separate savings account or Health Savings Account (if eligible) can help you manage these costs without impacting your core retirement savings.

Staying Physically Fit and Mentally Sharp

Retirement is the perfect time to focus on your well-being, and staying active both physically and mentally can improve your quality of life and even extend it. Here are some practical ways to incorporate health and fitness into your daily routine.

1. **Regular Exercise**

Aim to include a mix of aerobic, strength, and flexibility exercises in your routine. Activities like walking, swimming, or cycling are great for cardiovascular health, while resistance exercises (like using light weights or resistance bands) can maintain muscle strength. Flexibility and balance exercises, such as stretching is also valuable for reducing fall risks. Engage in a health and fitness routine fit for your health and advice by a medical personnel.

2. Healthy Nutrition

A balanced diet becomes increasingly important as we age. Focus on nutrient-dense foods, including vegetables, fruits, lean proteins, and whole grains. Consider reducing processed foods and added sugars, as these can contribute to chronic conditions like diabetes or heart disease. Staying hydrated is equally important for energy and mental clarity.

3. Stay Mentally Active

Keeping your mind sharp can improve your overall well-being and lower your risk of cognitive decline. Engage in activities that challenge your brain, such as puzzles, reading, games like chess or learning a new skill. Social interaction is also beneficial, so consider joining a local club, taking a class, or volunteering.

4. Prioritize Sleep and Stress Management

Quality sleep and stress management are crucial for both physical and mental health. Aim for 7-8 hours of restful sleep each night and develop routines that help you unwind. Techniques like meditation, deep breathing, or simply taking time each day for a quiet activity can reduce stress, improve mood, and enhance your immune system.

Preparing for Long-Term Care Needs

Long-term care involves services that help with everyday activities, like bathing, dressing, and eating, if you're no longer able to perform these tasks independently. Planning for long-term care can help you avoid significant financial strain and ensure you receive quality care when it's needed.

1. Understand What Long-Term Care Covers
Long-term care includes a range of services, from in-home assistance to nursing home care. Unlike standard health insurance, Medicare generally doesn't cover long-term care, making it essential to plan separately for these expenses.

2. Explore Long-Term Care Insurance
Long-term care insurance is designed to cover services that Medicare doesn't, such as personal and custodial care. Policies vary widely in terms of what they cover, so it's important to shop around, compare premiums, and review the fine print to make sure the policy aligns with your needs and budget. Some policies also offer inflation protection, which is worth considering to keep up with rising costs over time.

3. Consider Alternatives Like Hybrid Policies
Hybrid policies combine life insurance or annuities with long-term care coverage, offering a way to receive long-term care benefits if needed or leave a death benefit to heirs if not. This option can provide flexibility and ensure your premiums aren't lost if you never require long-term care.

4. Discuss Options with Family and Plan Ahead

If you have family members you'll rely on for care, it's important to have an open conversation about your expectations and preferences. Decide ahead of time what kind of care you'd prefer (in-home, assisted living, etc.) and make sure any necessary paperwork, such as healthcare directives or powers of attorney, are in place.

5. Set Aside Funds for Long-Term Care Expenses

Even if you don't purchase insurance, it's wise to budget for potential long-term care expenses. Setting aside a specific portion of your savings, or creating a dedicated account, can provide a financial cushion if you need to pay for in-home help or assisted living down the line.

Planning for health and longevity allows you to make the most of your retirement with confidence, knowing you're prepared for the expected and unexpected alike.

Chapter 5

Crafting Your Legacy of Impact and Purpose

Building a legacy isn't just about wealth; it's about the values, lessons, and impact you leave behind. Retirement is a perfect opportunity to look at what you want to be remembered for and how you want to shape the lives of those around you.

Passing on Your Values and Stories

One of the most powerful gifts you can leave is the wisdom gained from your life's experiences. Your stories, values, and life lessons can become a compass for your loved ones, guiding them through their own journeys.

1. Document Your Life Lessons

Consider recording or writing down the stories that defined you—moments of challenge, triumph, and even humor. These stories carry your values and unique perspective. Whether it's a funny anecdote about a career mishap or a deeply personal reflection on what family means to you, sharing these stories can create a lasting, personal connection with future generations.

2. Have Open Conversations with Family

Discuss the values you hold dear and why they matter to you. You might even organize regular family gatherings where you talk about personal goals, dreams, or ways each member can give back. These conversations foster a deeper understanding of each other's values and create lasting memories. You're not only sharing your beliefs—you're also building a legacy of open communication.

3. Create Meaningful Traditions

Another powerful way to pass on your values is through family traditions. Start annual gatherings, volunteer as a family for a cause you care about, or establish rituals that celebrate important milestones. Traditions bind families together, giving your loved ones something special to continue and cherish long after you're gone.

Making a Difference in Your Community

A significant part of crafting a legacy of impact is contributing to the world around you. Retirement provides the time and opportunity to deepen your involvement in causes you're passionate about, building connections and bringing positive change to your community.

1. Engage in Volunteer Work

Find causes that resonate with you and give back through volunteering. Whether you're interested in supporting education, the environment, or healthcare, there are countless ways to get involved. Volunteering isn't just about helping others; it also brings fulfillment and purpose, allowing you to make a tangible difference in the lives of those around you.

2. Mentor and Share Your Expertise

Retirement is an ideal time to share your skills and knowledge. Mentoring younger people in your field or community can have a lasting impact, helping the next generation gain confidence and skills. Consider offering your experience through mentorship programs, local schools, or community centers. Your guidance can inspire others to pursue their dreams and navigate challenges with resilience.

3. Create a Community Project

If there's a cause you feel strongly about, consider starting a project that reflects your passions. This could be anything from organizing a neighborhood clean-up to supporting local artists or setting up a scholarship fund. Creating a project is a meaningful way to make a difference, and it leaves a positive mark on your community, ensuring that your values live on through your efforts.

Giving Back: Charitable Contributions and Lasting Impact

Charitable giving is a powerful way to ensure your legacy makes a difference long after you're gone.

1. Choose Causes that Reflect Your Passions

Think about the issues you care most about—whether it's education, healthcare, the arts, or environmental conservation. By identifying a cause that's close to your heart, you make your charitable giving more meaningful and focused. Donating to organizations that reflect your passions adds a layer of personal connection, transforming your contributions into an expression of who you are.

2. Consider a Donor-Advised Fund or Community Foundation

If you're looking to make a significant impact, explore options like donor-advised funds or community foundations. These funds allow you to make charitable donations now, with the flexibility to choose specific organizations later. A donor-advised fund gives you control and lets you direct contributions to causes that emerge over time, adapting to new challenges or changes in your interests.

3. Inspire Future Generations with Charitable Traditions

Establish a tradition of giving that involves your family. For example, you could make annual donations in each family member's name or ask them to choose a charity that's meaningful to them. This approach doesn't just support worthy causes; it also teaches the importance of generosity and encourages your loved ones to carry on a legacy of giving.

Crafting a legacy of impact and purpose is an incredibly rewarding part of retirement. It allows you to reflect on what matters most, build meaningful connections, and leave a positive mark on the lives of others. Whether through sharing your stories, engaging in community work, or giving back to meaningful causes, the legacy you build reflects the life you lived and the values you cherished.

Chapter 6

Freedom, Fun, and Fulfillment in Retirement

Retirement is more than an end to work; it's the beginning of a whole new adventure. Now you have the freedom to follow your curiosity, dive into hobbies, give back to your community, or even see the world on your own schedule. This chapter is all about embracing the endless opportunities of retirement, from discovering passions to creating a lifestyle filled with purpose, joy, and connection.

Exploring New Passions and Hobbies

Retirement gives you the chance to rediscover what brings you joy. Maybe there's something you always wanted to try but never had the time. Now, the clock is on your side.

1. Reconnect with Old Interests

Think back to activities you loved in your youth or hobbies you had to set aside for work and family. Whether it's painting, gardening, playing an instrument, or getting back on the golf course, reconnecting with old interests can bring a sense of joy and comfort. These activities also remind you of the passions that have always been part of you.

2. Try Something Completely New

Retirement is the perfect time to try things you've never done before. Take a cooking class, learn to play chess, or experiment with photography. It's never too late to pick up a new hobby, and engaging in something fresh keeps the mind active and adds excitement to your days. There's something uniquely rewarding about being a beginner, learning for the joy of it, and discovering hidden talents along the way.

3. Engage in Creative Arts

Creative outlets like writing, painting, woodworking, or knitting offer an enjoyable way to express yourself. Creativity also has a therapeutic effect, reducing stress and bringing a sense of accomplishment. Plus, you can share your creations with family and friends, making your hobby a source of joy for others, too.

4. Stay Active with a Physical Hobby

Physical activities like hiking, dancing, or swimming can boost both your physical and mental health. Try joining a local club or class that offers group activities for older adults. Not only do you get to stay active, but you also make new friends who share your interests, adding a social element to your routine.

Reinventing Yourself with Part-Time Work or Volunteering

Just because you're retired doesn't mean you have to stop working if it's something you enjoy. Retirement is a chance to shift gears and perhaps explore a different kind of work—something that's meaningful, low-stress, and enjoyable. Or, you might find fulfillment through volunteering, sharing your skills and experience to make a difference.

1. Pursue Part-Time or Freelance Work

Retirement opens the door to exploring work on your own terms. You could find a part-time role in a field that interests you, take on consulting work in your area of expertise, or even start a small business based on a passion project. Working part-time allows you to stay engaged, add a little extra income, and meet new people—all without the demands of a full-time job.

2. Consider Mentorship or Teaching

With decades of experience, you have valuable knowledge to share. Many retirees find great fulfillment in mentoring or teaching, whether it's guiding young people in their careers, helping small business owners, or leading community workshops. Mentorship brings purpose to retirement, and knowing that your insights are helping others grow is incredibly rewarding.

3. Volunteer for Causes You Care About

Volunteering is a wonderful way to give back and make a positive impact. Choose a cause that resonates with you, whether it's supporting veterans, helping in local schools, working with animals, or assisting at a food bank. Volunteering not only allows you to stay active and connected but also lets you contribute to a greater good, adding a layer of meaning to your days.

4. Blend Travel with Purpose

For those who love to travel, consider "voluntourism"—a blend of volunteering and tourism. This option allows you to explore new places while giving back. You might help with conservation efforts, teach English, or assist with community projects in a location you've always wanted to visit.

Traveling Without a Time Clock: Adventures for the Free Spirit

One of the greatest freedoms in retirement is the ability to travel on your own schedule. There's no need to squeeze trips into a week's vacation—now you can explore at your own pace. Whether it's a long-desired cross-country road trip, visiting family across the globe, or a peaceful getaway to a quiet beach, retirement opens the world to you.

1. Take Your Time and Savor Each Destination

Without the rush of work deadlines, you can truly immerse yourself in each place you visit. Spend a few weeks in a single location to explore like a local, savoring the culture, food, and experiences. Staying longer allows you to discover the hidden gems that quick trips often miss.

2. Embrace the Joy of Spontaneity

With no tight schedules, you're free to be spontaneous. Maybe you want to take a road trip with no set plan, exploring as you go. Or perhaps you'd like to hop on a last-minute cruise or book a bed and breakfast in a nearby town. Retirement gives you the flexibility to follow your whims and enjoy the thrill of adventure without a rigid itinerary.

3. Explore "Senior-Friendly" Travel Options

Many travel companies offer packages tailored to older adults, making trips more comfortable and accessible. Consider small-group tours or cruises that handle the details for you, allowing you to focus on the experience. These tours often cater to specific interests, like history, wine tasting, or photography, letting you enjoy your travels without the stress of planning every detail.

4. Consider Extended Stays or Travel for Hobbies

With retirement's flexibility, you might enjoy an extended stay somewhere you love. Rent a cabin for a month in the mountains, spend a season in a coastal town, or travel to an area known for your favorite hobby, like a fishing village or art community. Extended stays offer a "home away from home" experience, letting you build connections and savor each moment without rushing.

Embrace the Freedom

Retirement is a unique chapter that gives you the freedom to write each day as you wish. It's a time to explore, grow, connect, and enjoy life with renewed passion. By finding hobbies that fulfill you, giving back in ways that inspire you, and exploring the world without limits, you're crafting a retirement that's meaningful, joyful, and uniquely yours.

Chapter 7

Strengthening Family Ties

Retirement is the perfect opportunity to deepen your relationships with family. With fewer time constraints, you can focus on creating meaningful connections, passing down your wisdom, and building a legacy that will live on through your loved ones. We are going to make reference to chapter 5 of this book. Let's take a step!

Becoming a Mentor: Sharing Your Wisdom with the Next Generation

One of the most valuable gifts you can give is the knowledge and wisdom you've gathered over the years. The younger generation, whether it's your children, grandchildren, nieces, nephews, or even family friends, can benefit from your experiences and guidance. Here's how to step into the role of a mentor in ways that feel natural and enjoyable.

1. Share Stories with Life Lessons

Younger family members might not always be open to "advice," but they love stories! Share anecdotes from your life that highlight important lessons—like the value of hard work, the importance of kindness, or a time when a failure turned into a valuable lesson. These stories make life's ups and downs feel relatable and can inspire them to persevere through their own challenges.

2. Teach Practical Skills

Think about the practical skills you can pass down, from financial basics and car maintenance to cooking family recipes or home repairs. Set aside time to teach them hands-on, making it a fun experience rather than a lecture. For example, you could have a "cooking day" with your grandkids, showing them how to make a favorite family dish. Skills like these don't just help them in life; they build confidence and create lasting memories.

3. Be Available for One-on-One Chats

Life can be confusing, especially for young adults. Let them know they can come to you with questions or just talk about life, relationships, career choices, and dreams. Be a listening ear without judgment, and let them know you're there to support them as they navigate their own paths. Sometimes, knowing they have someone they can count on for genuine advice makes a world of difference.

Grandparenting Goals: Making Memories that Last

If you're a grandparent, you know that grandkids bring a special kind of joy. Building a close bond with them not only enriches your life but also gives them a strong sense of family and belonging. Here are some fun and impactful ways to create memories that will stay with them forever.

1. Create Special "Grandparent Days"

Designate a specific day each month for a "grandparent day," where it's all about spending quality time together. Whether it's going to the park, watching their favorite movie, or doing a craft project, these regular dates give you a chance to bond and create traditions. Plus, it gives the kids something to look forward to each month!

2. Share Your Hobbies and Passions

Introduce your grandkids to the hobbies you love, whether it's fishing, baking, gardening, or woodworking. Kids love learning hands-on activities, especially when it's something unique. Not only will you be teaching them a new skill, but you're also passing on a part of yourself. Who knows—maybe you'll even discover a shared passion!

3. Capture Moments with a "Grandparent Journal"

Keep a journal or scrapbook dedicated to your time together. Jot down funny things they say, document special days, and include photos or little mementos. You can let the kids help decorate it, adding their drawings or notes. This journal becomes a treasure chest of memories they can look back on as they grow older, and it serves as a beautiful reminder of the special bond you share.

4. Be Present, Listen, and Show Unconditional Love

Kids thrive on positive attention. Sometimes, all they need is for you to be fully present, listening to their stories, their questions, and their dreams. Make them feel valued and understood, showing them they have a safe, loving space with you. This simple, consistent presence creates a powerful bond and leaves them with a lasting sense of love and security.

Building Connection through Family Traditions and Celebrations

Family traditions and celebrations bring everyone together, creating a sense of continuity and joy that spans generations. These traditions don't have to be extravagant; it's the togetherness that matters. Here are some ways to build traditions and plan celebrations that keep your family connected, no matter how much time passes.

1. Create Simple, Repeatable Traditions

Traditions can be as simple as making pancakes together every Sunday, having a family game night once a month, or organizing an annual "family Olympics" in the backyard. These small, repeatable activities bring everyone together and create shared memories that family members will look forward to year after year.

2. Celebrate Milestones and Achievements

Make it a family tradition to celebrate each person's big (and little) milestones. From graduations and job promotions to finishing a big project or learning a new skill, these small celebrations show everyone that they're valued and supported. Organizing a dinner, giving a handwritten note, or even hosting a small gathering can make a lasting impact on the person being celebrated.

3. Capture Holidays with Meaningful Rituals

Each holiday brings a chance to gather and make special memories. You might create a Thanksgiving gratitude circle, decorate together during the holidays, or organize a yearly family photo day. These rituals bring a sense of unity and joy, giving everyone a reason to come together and reconnect.

4. Build a Family Time Capsule

Get the whole family involved in creating a time capsule filled with letters, photos, and little items that represent the current year. Each family member can contribute something meaningful, and you can bury or store it with a plan to open it in the future. A family time capsule is a wonderful way to celebrate togetherness and preserve memories for the years to come.

5. Leave a Legacy of Connection

The beauty of these traditions and celebrations is that they create a legacy of connection and love. Each gathering, each shared experience, builds a web of memories that binds the family together, giving everyone a sense of belonging and security. These moments leave a lasting impact on each family member, ensuring that the bonds you've built remain strong even as life changes.

Strengthening family ties in retirement is one of the most rewarding ways to spend this phase of life. Through mentoring, grandparenting, and building family traditions, you're investing in the people who matter most. These bonds, built on love, shared memories, and meaningful connections, create a legacy that enriches your family and brings you fulfillment, joy, and a lasting sense of purpose.

Chapter 8

Managing Your Mental and Emotional Well-Being

Retirement brings the gift of time, but it also requires a new balance in mental and emotional well-being. Without the routines of work, it's easy to feel unanchored or isolated. These steps are not just about feeling good; they're about building a lifestyle that brings fulfillment and peace.

Finding Purpose and Joy in Everyday Moments

One of the keys to mental well-being is finding purpose. Purpose doesn't have to mean big goals; it can be found in the small moments of daily life, creating a sense of meaning that keeps you excited to wake up each day.

1. Set Daily Intentions

Each morning, set a small intention for the day. It could be as simple as, "Today, I'm going to enjoy my coffee slowly" or "I'll take a walk and really notice the nature around me." These intentions create a purpose for the day, no matter how small. It's about bringing more presence to your activities, allowing you to savor even the simplest moments.

2. Find Joy in Routine Activities

Embrace the rhythm of everyday tasks like cooking, gardening, or even tidying up. These activities, when done mindfully, can bring satisfaction and a surprising amount of joy. For example, if you love cooking, try a new recipe each week or cook a meal with a family member. It turns the ordinary into something fulfilling.

3. Explore Hobbies with Curiosity

Delve into hobbies that excite you. Maybe it's painting, writing, birdwatching, or even learning a new language. Approach each activity with curiosity rather than pressure. Hobbies allow you to lose track of time and give your mind a healthy, joyful focus. Trying something new can bring an added spark to your day and keep life interesting.

4. Celebrate Small Wins

Recognize and celebrate your achievements, no matter how small they may seem. Completed a book? Mastered a new dish? Organized the garage? Each small win is a reminder that you're moving forward and growing. This acknowledgment brings positivity and keeps you motivated.

Managing Stress and Embracing New Rhythms

While retirement can reduce work-related stress, new sources of stress can emerge. Shifting into a slower rhythm is an adjustment, but it can become deeply rewarding with a few simple techniques.

1. Establish a Flexible Routine

Create a loose daily structure that gives your day rhythm without feeling overly regimented. For instance, start with a morning walk or stretch, enjoy lunch at a set time, and make space in the evening for reflection or reading. This routine creates balance while leaving room for spontaneity, giving your day a comfortable flow.

2. Practice Mindfulness or Meditation

Practicing mindfulness helps you stay grounded and reduces stress. Try setting aside a few minutes each day for simple breathing exercises or meditation. Apps or online videos can help guide you. Regular mindfulness can bring calm and focus, helping you handle stress and find peace in the present moment.

3. Accept New Rhythms with Patience

Moving from a fast-paced career to a slower rhythm can be challenging. It's normal to feel unsettled at first. Remind yourself that it's okay to take things slow, to explore without a set destination. This is your time to relax and rediscover yourself. Let go of the need to always "do" and embrace the chance to simply "be."

4. Keep Moving Physically

Physical activity is a fantastic stress reliever and boosts mental well-being. Whether it's a daily walk, gentle yoga, or even dancing in the living room, moving your body releases endorphins and reduces stress. Make physical activity a natural part of your day, helping you stay fit and energized.

Staying Connected: Friendships, Community, and Social Life

Social connections are essential for mental and emotional health, especially in retirement when you may not have the built-in social network of a workplace. Strengthening existing relationships and finding new connections can bring a sense of belonging, joy, and companionship.

1. Make Time for Friends

Reach out to friends you may not have had time to connect with regularly. Plan simple outings like a coffee date, a movie night, or a shared walk. These moments don't need to be elaborate; it's about enjoying each other's company and building shared memories. Staying connected with friends adds a social rhythm to your life, keeping loneliness at bay.

2. Get Involved in Community Activities

Community activities are a wonderful way to meet new people and become a part of something bigger. Look for local classes, social groups, or clubs that focus on your interests. You might join a book club, take a painting class, or volunteer for local projects. Community involvement brings a sense of purpose and introduces you to new, like-minded friends.

3. Host Family or Neighborhood Gatherings

Invite family or neighbors over for simple gatherings. Whether it's a casual potluck, a game night, or just tea on the porch, these gatherings build connections in a relaxed setting. Make it a tradition, perhaps a monthly get-together, that strengthens bonds and creates joyful social moments.

4. Find Supportive Online Communities

If in-person meetups aren't always possible, online communities can provide meaningful connection, too. Look for forums, social media groups, or virtual classes centered around your hobbies or interests. You can join a virtual book club, participate in online workshops, or simply chat with others who share your passions. These connections can be surprisingly fulfilling, offering support and friendship.

5. Be Open to New Friendships

Retirement often brings the opportunity to meet people from diverse backgrounds and experiences. Be open to forming friendships with people of all ages and backgrounds. You might discover that sharing perspectives with people different from yourself brings fresh insights and a sense of camaraderie. Embracing new friendships enriches your life and keeps you engaged with the world around you.

By finding purpose, managing stress, and nurturing social connections, you can build a retirement filled with mental and emotional well-being. Every day offers the chance to savor life's small joys, share moments with loved ones, and embrace a rhythm that brings peace and contentment. This stage of life is a gift!!!

Chapter 9

Navigating Unexpected Changes with Confidence

Retirement is a time of freedom and joy, but it can also bring unexpected changes. Financial markets fluctuate, personal losses occur, and health challenges may arise. By preparing mentally and practically, you can face these surprises with resilience and confidence.

Adapting to Financial Market Fluctuations

Retirement savings are often invested in markets that can be unpredictable. While market fluctuations are normal, they can feel unsettling, especially when you're no longer adding new income. Learning to manage your investments wisely and stay calm through the ups and downs can protect your financial health and peace of mind.

1. Diversify Your Investments for Stability

Diversification means spreading your investments across different types of assets (like stocks, bonds, and real estate) to reduce risk. By not putting "all your eggs in one basket," you create a balance that can handle market shifts more smoothly. A diversified portfolio can keep your savings steady, even if one part of the market takes a downturn. Talk to a financial advisor about adjusting your investments to match your retirement needs and risk tolerance.

2. Maintain a "Safety Net" Fund

Having a separate "safety net" or emergency fund in cash or short-term bonds allows you to cover living expenses without touching your main investments during market dips. This fund acts as a cushion, giving you the flexibility to wait for your investments to recover before withdrawing from them. Aim for 6-12 months' worth of living expenses in this account.

3. Stay Calm and Avoid Rash Decisions

When markets drop, it's tempting to react by selling investments to avoid further losses. However, this can lock in losses that could otherwise recover over time. Instead, remind yourself that markets historically rebound after downturns. Avoid checking your investments daily—consider reviewing them quarterly or yearly. If you feel worried, talk to your advisor before making any sudden changes.

4. Consider a Withdrawal Strategy

Plan your withdrawals thoughtfully to minimize the impact of market fluctuations on your savings. One approach is the "bucket strategy," where you keep funds for immediate expenses in cash or bonds while allowing other investments to grow. By pulling from your safest assets during market lows, you avoid selling growth-focused assets when their value is temporarily down.

Handling Personal Loss and Health Challenges

Retirement brings more time to enjoy life, but it's also a phase where personal losses and health issues may emerge. While these moments can be deeply challenging, preparing in advance can help you approach them with strength and self-compassion.

1. Plan for Healthcare Needs Early

Make sure you have a healthcare plan that includes insurance coverage for unexpected needs. Review your insurance options and consider supplemental plans if needed. Staying proactive with regular check-ups and screenings also helps you catch issues early and stay healthy.

2. Build a Support Network

Surrounding yourself with family, friends, and even community groups can make all the difference when facing loss or health issues. Don't be afraid to reach out to your loved ones and let them know when you need support. Build connections with neighbors, faith groups, or local organizations that offer companionship and practical help.

3. Practice Self-Compassion During Loss

Losing a loved one or dealing with illness can be overwhelming. Give yourself permission to grieve, feel, and heal at your own pace. Sometimes people feel pressured to "stay strong," but allowing yourself to process emotions is healthier in the long run. You might find it helpful to write in a journal, talk to a therapist, or join a support group where others understand what you're going through.

4. Stay Physically Active to Boost Well-Being

Regular physical activity can enhance both physical and mental health, helping you stay resilient in tough times. Even gentle exercise like walking, stretching, or yoga can improve mood, reduce stress, and keep your body strong. Aim to make movement a daily habit, and listen to your body's needs, especially during challenging moments.

Building Resilience and Embracing Life's Ups and Downs

Life is full of unexpected twists, even in retirement. Learning to face these changes with resilience can turn challenges into opportunities for personal growth. Embracing life's ups and downs with a flexible mindset helps you adapt and find peace in every stage.

1. Cultivate a Positive Perspective

Resilience often starts with a positive outlook. Rather than seeing challenges as obstacles, try to view them as opportunities to grow. When facing a tough situation, ask yourself, "What can I learn from this?" or "How can I become stronger through this experience?" Adopting a growth mindset can help you find meaning and strength even in difficult times.

2. Practice Gratitude Daily

Gratitude is a powerful tool for building resilience. Each day, take a moment to reflect on things you're grateful for, whether it's a conversation with a friend, a beautiful sunset, or a new hobby you've discovered. Gratitude helps shift focus away from stress and fosters a positive, hopeful outlook, even when life feels uncertain.

3. Find Comfort in Routine and Flexibility

A simple daily routine can offer comfort and stability. At the same time, it's helpful to stay open to change. Life in retirement doesn't always go as planned, and learning to be flexible can make adjustments easier. Build a routine but allow space for spontaneity or new experiences that bring joy and fulfillment.

4. Connect with Nature for Peace and Perspective

Nature has a calming effect, reminding us of life's natural rhythms. Take regular walks outdoors, garden, or spend time by a body of water. Engaging with nature offers perspective, helping you feel connected to something larger than yourself and reminding you that change is part of life.

5. Reflect on Your Legacy and Purpose

Challenging times can deepen your understanding of what really matters. Use these moments to reflect on your purpose, values, and the legacy you want to leave behind. Retirement gives you the time to explore these big questions, and by focusing on what brings you meaning, you'll find strength even when life is unpredictable.

Navigating life's changes in retirement requires a balance of preparation, flexibility, and self-compassion. By planning financially, building support systems, and nurturing your inner resilience, you can handle unexpected challenges with confidence.

Chapter 10

The Ultimate Retirement Bucket List

Retirement isn't just about slowing down; it's a time to embrace new adventures and discover what makes life truly fulfilling. Whether you dream of traveling the world, learning a new skill, or simply spending more time with loved ones, creating a personalized bucket list can add excitement and meaning to each day.

Crafting Your Personalized Adventure Plan

A bucket list isn't just a random collection of goals; it's a roadmap that reflects who you are, what excites you, and the experiences that bring you joy. The first step in creating your list is to dive deep into what matters most to you. This plan can be as adventurous or as laid-back as you want—it's all about making sure each item aligns with your values and dreams.

1. Reflect on Your Passions and Interests

Think about the activities, places, and experiences that have always intrigued you. Is there a hobby you've always wanted to try, a country you've longed to visit, or a skill you'd like to develop? Start by jotting down anything that excites you, big or small. This could range from visiting a national park to learning to play the guitar, or even spending a month in a different city.

2. Set Realistic but Inspiring Goals

Your bucket list should inspire you but also feel achievable. Break down big dreams into smaller, actionable steps. For instance, if "Write a memoir" feels overwhelming, start with "Write one chapter each month." Creating a mix of short-term and long-term goals adds variety and makes each step enjoyable.

3. Prioritize Experiences over Possessions

Research shows that experiences bring more lasting happiness than material items. As you create your list, focus on memories and adventures rather than possessions. Prioritize experiences that bring you joy, like attending a concert, hiking a scenic trail, or taking a road trip. These moments become treasured memories and give you a deeper sense of satisfaction.

4. Add a Mix of Comfort and Challenge

Retirement is a great time to embrace both the familiar and the unknown. Include some items that you know will bring joy—such as a favorite pastime or visiting family—and a few that push you outside your comfort zone. Trying something new can be energizing, whether it's a creative project, a new language, or an adventurous outing. This blend keeps life exciting and enriching.

5. Consider Travel and Exploration

Travel is a common bucket list item, but it doesn't have to mean far-off destinations. While international trips are wonderful, there's also beauty in exploring nearby towns, national parks, or historical sites. Plan according to your interests, whether it's scenic train journeys, local festivals, or visiting family members across the country. Every trip, big or small, can bring a sense of discovery and wonder.

Meaningful Goals and Experiences to Look Forward To

A bucket list should add meaning and purpose to your retirement years. Beyond just "doing things," think about goals that enrich your life and bring a sense of accomplishment.

1. Pursue Lifelong Learning

Retirement is an ideal time to explore new topics and skills. Whether you've always wanted to paint, learn to cook exotic dishes, or take a history course, education can be both rewarding and fulfilling. Many universities and online platforms offer courses for seniors, often at reduced rates, allowing you to keep your mind active and engaged.

2. Engage in Community or Volunteering

Making a positive impact can be one of the most fulfilling aspects of retirement. Consider adding volunteer work to your list, especially if it aligns with a cause you're passionate about, like environmental conservation, education, or animal welfare. Volunteering doesn't only benefit others; it enriches your own life by fostering connections, giving back, and bringing a sense of purpose.

3. Create "Family and Friends" Goals

Building memories with family and friends can be deeply satisfying. Plan special events, like family reunions, monthly brunches, or trips with grandchildren. Create goals around capturing these moments, such as a "Family Photo Day" or recording family stories in a memory book. These experiences strengthen bonds and create lasting memories that mean more than any material gift.

4. Prioritize Health and Wellness Goals

Staying active and healthy enhances both physical and mental well-being. Your bucket list might include trying a new fitness routine, completing a local 5K, or taking up a hobby like tai chi or swimming. Wellness also includes relaxation goals like meditation retreats or spa days. By focusing on your health, you ensure that you can enjoy your adventures with energy and vitality.

5. Make Time for Personal Reflection and Growth

Personal growth doesn't stop in retirement. Set goals that help you reflect on your life and gain a deeper understanding of yourself. This could include activities like journaling, meditation, or even writing a memoir. Reflecting on your values, beliefs, and life experiences not only brings clarity but also creates a sense of peace and fulfillment.

Achieving Life Satisfaction on Your Terms

The beauty of retirement is the freedom to create a life that aligns with your values, pace, and personal dreams. By focusing on what brings you joy and satisfaction, your bucket list becomes a tool for achieving a well-rounded, happy retirement. Here are ways to stay motivated and ensure you're living life fully on your own terms.

1. Take Small Steps Regularly

Big dreams are accomplished one small step at a time. Break down your bucket list items into manageable actions, and set aside time each week or month to work toward them. For example, if your goal is to learn to paint, start with a weekly art class. Celebrate each milestone, and keep a journal to track your progress.

2. Be Flexible and Open to New Ideas

Life doesn't always go as planned, and that's okay. Allow yourself to change your goals as new interests emerge or as you experience different things. Flexibility lets you adjust your bucket list to fit your current desires, keeping it fresh and exciting. You might even stumble upon unexpected adventures that bring more joy than what you originally planned.

3. Involve Loved Ones in Your Adventures

Many experiences become richer when shared. Invite family and friends to join you on trips, classes, or simple outings. Sharing your goals and dreams can motivate you and strengthen your relationships. Even something as simple as a monthly coffee date or an annual family trip adds fulfillment and companionship to your journey.

4. Balance Adventure with Relaxation

While it's wonderful to explore, don't forget to include moments of relaxation. Balance your bucket list with activities that recharge you, like reading a book, spending a quiet afternoon in nature, or taking a day to unwind at home. Retirement is a time to enjoy both the thrill of adventure and the peace of rest.

5. Embrace a Grateful Mindset

Gratitude enhances life satisfaction by helping you focus on the positive. Regularly reflect on the experiences you've achieved, and appreciate the moments that bring you joy. Keep a gratitude journal, noting both big accomplishments and small joys. This practice can deepen your appreciation for the life you're creating and remind you of all you've accomplished.

6. Celebrate Your Milestones

Each time you check something off your bucket list, celebrate it! This might be as simple as sharing the moment with a loved one, enjoying a favorite meal, or giving yourself a small reward. Celebrating your accomplishments reinforces your progress, keeping you motivated to pursue your next adventure.

The ultimate retirement bucket list is about more than crossing items off a list; it's about filling your life with purpose, joy, and meaningful moments. This is your time to explore, grow, and create a legacy of experiences that truly matter to you. By crafting a plan that reflects your passions, setting meaningful goals, and celebrating each step, you're building a retirement that's deeply fulfilling and uniquely yours.

Chapter 11

Financial Checklist for a Secure Future

A secure financial foundation allows you to enjoy retirement without the stress of financial worries. While you may have already done the bulk of your planning, keeping your finances on track requires ongoing attention. By setting up a yearly financial review, being mindful of key age-related milestones, and building flexibility into your plans, you can enjoy the years ahead with confidence and peace of mind.

Reviewing Your Financial Health Yearly
A yearly financial check-up helps you stay aware of where you stand, spot any changes that might be needed, and stay aligned with your goals. This review doesn't need to be complicated; a simple but thorough approach can make a big difference in your peace of mind and financial security.

1. Revisit Your Budget and Spending Habits
Start by reviewing your budget and monthly spending. Are you sticking to your planned budget, or have your expenses changed? Look for areas where you might be spending more or less than anticipated. If costs for items like healthcare or leisure activities have shifted, adjust

your budget accordingly to ensure it reflects your current lifestyle.

2. Assess Your Income Sources

Go over your retirement income sources, including Social Security, pensions, and investment withdrawals. Confirm that each source is still meeting your needs and check whether any adjustments are needed. For example, you might want to increase or decrease withdrawals based on your spending. Tracking your income streams keeps you prepared for any changes that might affect your monthly cash flow.

3. Review Your Investments

Take a close look at your investment portfolio to ensure it's aligned with your goals and risk tolerance. As you age, you may want to shift to more conservative investments, but this decision depends on your individual circumstances. Consider consulting with a financial advisor to help you determine if your asset allocation still makes sense for your needs and time horizon.

4. Update Insurance and Healthcare Plans

Healthcare needs can change from year to year, so it's wise to review your Medicare or private insurance coverage annually. Look into whether your plan still meets your needs or if adjustments are necessary, especially for prescription drug coverage or any new health conditions. If you have long-term care insurance, review the terms to ensure it continues to provide adequate coverage.

5. Check Your Emergency Fund

An emergency fund is essential for covering unexpected costs without dipping into your investments. Ensure your emergency savings are still sufficient, ideally covering 6-12 months of living expenses. If you've used any of it over the past year, prioritize replenishing it to stay prepared for the unexpected.

Key Milestones and Age-Based Planning Tips

As you progress through retirement, certain age-based milestones can impact your finances. Being aware of these key points allows you to make informed decisions and avoid penalties. This guide highlights the main financial milestones you may encounter.

1. Age 59½ – Penalty-Free Withdrawals

At this age, you can begin taking withdrawals from retirement accounts, like 401(k)s or IRAs, without the typical early withdrawal penalty. This flexibility can be helpful if you decide to retire early or need access to funds for specific expenses. However, be mindful that withdrawals are still subject to income tax.

2. Age 62 – Social Security Eligibility

Age 62 is the earliest you can claim Social Security benefits, though the amount will be lower than if you wait until full retirement age (FRA). Deciding when to claim depends on factors like your health, income needs, and other sources of income. Delaying benefits can increase your monthly payout, so weigh your options carefully.

3. Full Retirement Age (FRA) – Maximize Social Security

Your FRA, typically between 66 and 67 depending on your birth year, is when you can claim your full Social Security benefit. Waiting until this age avoids a reduction in benefits and may be a good choice if you don't need the income immediately. If you can, delaying even further to age 70 increases your monthly benefit significantly.

4. Age 70½ to 73 – Required Minimum Distributions (RMDs)

Once you reach 70½ (for older retirees) or 73 (for most current retirees), the IRS requires you to start taking RMDs from tax-deferred accounts like 401(k)s and IRAs. Failure to take your RMDs can result in significant penalties, so mark this milestone on your calendar. An annual review ensures you're on track and helps you avoid surprises when it's time to withdraw.

5. Annual Roth Conversion Opportunities

Each year, you have the opportunity to convert traditional IRA funds to a Roth IRA, where they grow tax-free. This strategy may benefit retirees in lower tax brackets, as it allows you to reduce future tax liabilities on retirement income. Consider consulting a tax professional to explore whether partial conversions might benefit you over the long term.

Maintaining Financial Flexibility and Security

Retirement brings a variety of expenses, so keeping your finances flexible ensures you're prepared for life's changes. Whether it's an unexpected expense or an opportunity for travel, flexibility helps you enjoy retirement without financial stress.

1. Establish a "Flexible Spending" Fund

Alongside your regular budget, consider setting aside a "flexible spending" fund for discretionary expenses like travel, hobbies, or family events. This fund allows you to embrace opportunities without tapping into your core retirement savings. By planning ahead, you'll have the freedom to say "yes" to experiences that enrich your life.

2. Consider a "Bucket" Strategy for Withdrawals

The "bucket" strategy divides your savings into different buckets based on time horizons and risk tolerance. For example, keep one bucket in cash or short-term bonds for immediate expenses, a second bucket in conservative investments for medium-term needs, and a third in growth-focused investments for long-term stability. This approach provides flexibility, allowing you to adapt withdrawals based on market conditions.

3. Be Strategic About Taxes

Taxes can significantly affect retirement income, so it's helpful to consider strategies that minimize your tax burden. For instance, you might withdraw from taxable accounts first, followed by tax-deferred accounts, to reduce overall taxes. Working with a tax professional can help you tailor these strategies to your unique situation, potentially extending the life of your savings.

4. Regularly Revisit Your Estate Plan

While estate planning may have been part of your initial retirement preparation, revisit it periodically to keep it up to date. This includes updating beneficiary designations, reviewing power of attorney, and making any adjustments to reflect changes in family or financial circumstances. Keeping your estate plan current adds peace of mind, ensuring that your wishes are honored.

5. Stay Informed and Adapt to Changes

The financial landscape changes over time, from tax laws to Medicare policies. Staying informed allows you to make the most of your benefits and avoid unexpected costs. Read up on changes that might affect your retirement or work with a financial advisor who can help you adapt your strategy as needed.

6. Maintain a Health Care Cushion

Health expenses can be a significant part of retirement, especially as you age. In addition to insurance, set aside extra savings specifically for healthcare needs, including potential long-term care. This additional cushion allows you to handle health expenses without compromising your lifestyle or pulling from core savings.

Building Confidence Through Preparation

A secure financial future in retirement requires more than just saving; it's about making consistent adjustments, staying informed, and ensuring that your plans reflect your evolving needs. By following this checklist each year, you stay proactive, prepared, and confident about your financial well-being.

Conclusion

Thriving in Your Golden Years

Retirement is a season of life that celebrates all you've accomplished, yet it's also a beginning—a time to embrace new passions, deepen relationships, and create moments of joy. As you step into this chapter, remember that every day is an opportunity to build the life you truly desire, with the freedom to explore, connect, and enjoy each moment.

Celebrating Your Achievements and Looking Forward
Take a moment to reflect on all that has led you to this stage: the career you've built, the family and friendships you've nurtured, and the countless ways you've impacted those around you. Each experience and accomplishment has shaped who you are today, and retirement gives you the freedom to celebrate these achievements while dreaming of what's yet to come. This is your time to live fully on your terms, free to choose the activities, goals, and experiences that bring you joy.

Retirement is not a destination; it's a dynamic journey that invites you to grow, adapt, and embrace the joys and surprises that lie ahead. By setting goals, staying connected with loved ones, and nurturing your health, you can build a life that continues to be meaningful and fulfilling. Look forward to the adventures waiting for you, knowing that every day offers the chance to discover something new about yourself and the world.

Finding Peace, Purpose, and Joy in Retirement

At its heart, a fulfilling retirement is about finding peace, purpose, and joy in the everyday moments. Whether it's a quiet morning with a cup of coffee, a walk in the park, a conversation with a friend, or pursuing a lifelong passion, true satisfaction comes from these simple, intentional experiences. Purpose, too, is found in all the ways you choose to give back, to stay connected, and to leave a legacy for those you care about.

As you embrace the rhythm of retirement, remember that joy is yours to cultivate each day. This stage is a gift—an invitation to live more freely, love more deeply, and appreciate the beauty around you. Your retirement years can be some of the most vibrant and fulfilling yet, as long as you approach each day with gratitude, curiosity, and an open heart.

So here's to you—celebrating the achievements that have brought you to this moment, embracing the freedom to pursue what brings you joy, and creating a legacy that reflects a life well-lived. May these golden years be filled with adventure, peace, and a deep sense of purpose. Your best years are not behind you; they're waiting for you right now, in every new day.

www.ingramcontent.com/pod-product-compliance
Lightning Source LLC
Chambersburg PA
CBHW070124230526
45472CB00004B/1401